Communication and Collaboration

Team Building Strategies for Success

Table of Contents

Coming together is a beginning, staying together is progress, and working together is success.

Chapter 1. Introduction

Are you ready to unlock the magic formula for effective and successful team collaboration? Our Special Report, "Communication and Collaboration: Team Building Strategies for Success," possesses an array of invaluable insights that will catapult your team into a new realm of productivity! Embark on an enriching journey through comprehensive strategies, authentic case studies, and groundbreaking communication techniques that have revived teams around the globe. This isn't just any report—it's your ticket to creating a harmonious, dynamic, and high-performing team! With any uncertainty swept away, it's time to leap into the rewarding world of exceptional teamwork. Don't miss your chance to propel your team to unprecedented heights—purchase your copy of the Special Report today!

Chapter 2. Understanding the Role of Communication in Team Success

Advancing through this chapter, we will delve into the essence of communication in enhancing teamwork. By defining key dimensions of communication, illustrating its significant role within a team setting, and reviewing the pronounced impacts on team success, we provide integral knowledge to appreciate the immeasurable value of communication within teams.

2.1. Understanding Different Dimensions of Communication

Communication is comprised of two core dimensions - verbal and nonverbal. Verbal communication, marked by spoken or written exchange of words, is essential for transmitting intricate ideas, tasks, and requests in a precise, unambiguous manner. Nonverbal communication, embodying body language, facial expressions, or tone of voice, may affirm or contrast verbal messages, and influences the interpretation and sentiment associated with conveyed messages. Both dimensions jointly shape the meaning and thematic undertone of communication, and their careful orchestration is paramount in preserving clarity, intention, and sentiment in team interactions.

2.2. Role of Communication in Team Cohesion

Consistent and clear communication serves as the adhesive binding team members together, reinforcing cohesion and camaraderie. A dependable system of communication promotes mutual understanding, creates a platform for idea exchange, and enables conflict resolution. Expression of opinions, feelings, and ideas opens the gate to empathy, fostering a supportive environment within the team. Transparency derived from open dialogue can bolster trust and reliance amongst team members, thereby amplifying team cohesion.

2.3. Impact of Communication on Task Clarity, Alignment, and Execution

Beyond fostering cohesion, communication plays an indispensable role in task alignment and execution. Clear communication of objectives, roles, responsibilities, and expectations is instrumental in shaping a shared understanding of the task at hand. By promoting alignment, it minimizes confusion and maximizes efficiency, eventually leading to superior task execution. Regular updates on task progress ensure everyone remains on the same page and facilitates swift course correction, when required. High-quality feedback using respectful language and constructive criticism reinforces learning and optimizes task execution over time.

2.4. Communication-Driven Decision Making

Within a team setting, effective communication protocols are vital to decision-making. Transparent sharing of information and ideas invites a diversity of perspectives, stimulating more comprehensive evaluation and resulting in well-informed decisions. Effective communication ensures broad consensus and minimizes misunderstanding amongst team members about key decisions, fostering aligned action and collective commitment.

2.5. Communication Facilitating Innovation and Problem Solving

The ability to communicate effectively has been identified as a key driver of innovation and problem solving. When team members feel heard and acknowledged, they are more likely to suggest fresh ideas or radical solutions. A respectful, open dialogue cultivates an environment where risk-taking is encouraged, creativity flourishes, and innovation thrives. Furthermore, effective communication helps to dissect complex problems, promoting collaborative problem solving and resulting in comprehensive, sustainable solutions.

2.6. Importance of Communication in Conflict Resolution

Inevitably teams will face conflicts; however, with effective communication, these can be transitioned into essential catalysts for learning and growth. Clear, empathetic communication plays a crucial role in illuminating different perspectives, acknowledging emotions, and negotiating solutions. The key lies in fostering an environment where concerns or disagreements can be voiced constructively and resolved amicably.

From the aforementioned exploration, it is evident that communication is the lifeblood for team success. Its ability to foster cohesion, clarify tasks, drive decision making, stimulate innovation, and resolve conflicts underlines its indispensable role within a team. A substantial investment in developing communication skills and systems can yield high dividends in terms of team success and productivity. It isn't an overestimation to declare that the success of a work team is, to a great extent, contingent on their collective proficiency in communication.

Chapter 3. Barriers to Effective Communication: Recognizing and Overcoming

Even in scenarios where everyone shares the identical ultimate goal, human communication can still be highly complex. Various barriers can impede effective communication, which in turn, affect collaboration and coordination in teams. Identifying these barriers and developing strategies to counteract them is indispensable in promoting a thriving and dynamic team environment.

3.1. Psychological Barriers

One of the most prevalent barriers to effective communication rests in our minds: psychological barriers. These can exist in various forms, such as fear, stress, low self-esteem, or negative emotions. For a team to reach an optimal level of functionality, it is essential to recognize and address these inhibitions.

Fear and anxiety can silence open dialogue, while chronic stress can significantly reduce cognitive functioning, leading to misinterpretations and false assumptions. Negative emotions like anger and frustration have a similar effect, leading to a breakdown of effective communication. In environments where low self-esteem is present, team members may not express their thoughts for fear of ridicule or dismissal. This silence curtails open communication, impeding team collaboration.

Mitigating these psychological barriers involves fostering a supportive team environment empathetic to mental stressors. Team-building exercises, mental health support initiatives, and a respectful, non-judgmental atmosphere are ways to counteract these barriers.

3.2. Cultural Barriers

As the workplace becomes increasingly multicultural, cultural barriers present a significant challenge to effective communication. Fundamental differences in languages, social norms, values, and expectations can induce misunderstandings and conflicts.

Overcoming cultural barriers requires a proactive, two-pronged approach. First, a strong foundation of cultural sensitivity and awareness should be established. This includes an encouragement of multicultural education, mutual respect, and understanding. Secondly, fostering an inclusive environment where all cultural backgrounds are valued and appreciated leads to a diversified and enriched team culture.

3.3. Organizational Barriers

Communication within a team doesn't function in isolation—it's influenced heavily by the larger organizational context. Factors like company policies, hierarchical structures, unclear job descriptions, or inadequate resources can obstruct effective team communication.

Tackling these barriers requires organizational changes, such as fine-tuning the organizational structure to encourage communication, improving clarity in job roles, and ensuring teams have the resources they need. A transparent system for transmitting information, explicitly declarative job roles, and an atmosphere that encourages questions and clarifications—all contribute to minimizing organizational barriers to communication.

3.4. Physical Barriers

In some instances, effective team communication is inhibited by logistical and physical roadblocks. Large distances between team members, inadequate facilities, or technical issues are some problems in this category. These barriers have become increasingly relevant with the rise of remote work, which introduces new challenges like time zone differences, virtual meeting limitations and technology malfunctions.

Physical barriers can be mitigated with the right technology and planning. Leveraging digital collaboration tools, prioritizing accessibility, clear protocols for virtual communication and effective time management strategies are crucial in combating these challenges.

3.5. Personal Barriers

Each team member brings unique communication styles and patterns that could either enhance or hamper the team's ability to communicate effectively. Some individuals are more introverted, while others may have a tendency to dominate conversations. Even individual biases and preconceived notions can act as barriers to a healthy exchange of ideas.

Overcoming personal barriers involves building a culture of respect and active listening. Acknowledging and valuing everyone's input, embracing a diversity of communication styles, understanding personal biases, and fostering an atmosphere of respectful dialogue—all contribute to overcoming personal barriers.

In conclusion, to overcome barriers to effective communication, it's vital first to identify them and understand their impact. Leveraging the right tactics—focused around empathy, respect, cultural awareness, organizational clarity, and effective use of technology—can move your team toward a more open and robust communication environment, propelling your team towards exceptional collaboration and productivity. This understanding and practice will bridge any existing communication gaps, fostering a healthier, dynamic, and successful team environment.

Chapter 4. Collaboration: The Heart of High-Performing Teams

At the core of every high-performing team, collaboration is the lifeblood that galvanizes disparate individuals into a cohesive, focused unit. It is the principal tool that amalgamates the myriad skills, ideas, and motivations represented within the team into a congruous entity, working seamlessly towards the accomplishment of shared objectives.

4.1. Understanding the Concept of Collaboration

Collaboration, in its purest form, is the act of working together to achieve a common goal. It often involves a melding of perspectives, ideas, and expertise, which is then synthesized into a collective output. Communication is the cornerstone of effective collaboration, acting as the connective thread that entwines individual offerings into a unified outcome.

However, collaboration is much more than the simple sharing of ideas. It is about creating a synergized atmosphere, where everyone feels respected, appreciated, and valued for their unique contributions. A team that embraces collaboration fosters a sense of belonging among its members, allowing for open dialogue, mutual respect, and proactive problem-solving.

4.2. The Five Pillars of Effective Collaboration

In dissecting the essence of fruitful collaboration, it's essential to illuminate the five pivotal pillars that underpin it.

1. **Shared Purpose:** Effective collaboration begins with the establishment of a shared purpose. This is the driving force that motivates each team member to contribute actively towards the attainment of the team goal.

2. **Trust and Openness:** Trust, transparency, and openness form the bedrock of successful collaboration. Team members must feel safe in expressing their ideas, exposing their vulnerabilities, and admitting their mistakes without fear of retribution.

3. **Potent Communication:** Communication is the lifeblood flowing through the arteries of collaboration. It's paramount to have clear, concise, and open lines of communication, enabling the exchange of ideas, thoughts, and feedback.

4. **Respect for Diversity:** An effective collaborative environment cherishes diversity and inclusivity. It is appreciative of each member's unique abilities, perspectives, and experiences, understanding the value they bring to the table.

5. **Consensus-Oriented Decision Making:** Teams that excel at collaboration prioritize consensus-oriented decision-making. This ensures that everyone's perspectives are heard and valued, fostering a sense of joint ownership and collective responsibility.

4.3. Keys to Promoting Collaboration in Teams

Accumulating knowledge about collaboration is valuable, but understanding how to apply this knowledge in real-world scenarios is crucial.

1. **Encourage Active Participation:** Engagement is the stepping stone for collaboration. Encouraging all team members to contribute their perspectives fosters an environment that promotes collaborative decision-making.

2. **Lead by Example:** As a leader, your actions set the tone for the team. By demonstrating collaborative behavior, you are effectively laying down the foundation for your team to emulate.

3. **Cultivate Empathetic Listening:** Empathetic listening goes beyond merely hearing words. It involves understanding the feelings, perceptions, and concerns behind the spoken words, which is vital in a collaborative environment.

4. **Build a Safe Space for Ideation:** Fostering a conducive environment for ideation encourages creativity, experimentation, and innovation - the life force behind competitive advantage.

4.4. The Impact of Collaboration on Team Dynamics

When collaboration becomes a default mode of operation within a team, profound changes happen. Collaboration has a direct impact on enhanced productivity, increased engagement, and the breeding of innovative ideas. Moreover, it promotes a sense of shared ownership and accountability, further bolstering the team's performance.

In summation, collaboration is not merely a strategy to achieve goals but an ethos that needs to permeate the team landscape. A team rooted in collaboration is a dynamic ensemble, rich with a diverse resonance of ideas, perspectives, and skills, all harmonized towards the realization of a shared vision. By fostering a collaborative environment, you are empowering your team to engage in a shared quest for excellence, nurturing not just a high-performing team but a cadre of fulfilled, engaged, and motivated individuals.

Chapter 5. Strategies to Foster Openness and Trust in Teams

Teams that function robustly are those where each member trusts one another. It is a landscape where openness and trust thrive, promoting optimal performance. To cultivate this conducive environment, certain strategies need to be employed.

5.1. Identifying the Role of Openness in Teams

Openness in a team encourages dialogue, cultivates creativity, and promotes problem-solving. Sharing of knowledge unfettered by fear enables a team to pull together their resources and skills to tackle the challenges that confront them. Openness fosters a "learning environment" that incessantly yearns for and assimilates new ideas and solutions. It encourages curiosity and the courage to question, paving the way for uninhibited innovation.

Crucially, openness drives accountability as well. When information and decisions are openly shared among members, everyone feels a shared responsibility for the consequences. Thus, openness has the power to drive individual contributions toward collective success.

5.2. Building Layers of Trust

Trust is a fundamental factor dividing high-performing teams from the rest. It mutes unnecessary noise, brings focus, and accelerates decisions. Trust seems simple, yet it is among the most challenging elements to build and maintain in a team. It springs from repeated experiences of reliability, competency, and empathy.

In fostering trust within teams, layers need to be meticulously built:

- Predictability: Team members should be able to predict each other's responses and actions. This base layer strengthens a sense of reliability.

- Value alignment: Mutual understanding and respecting each other's values form the next layer. It deepens the connection among the team, fostering a sense of belonging.

- Empathy: The top layer entails recognizing and understanding each other's emotions. It connects team members on a personal level, enhancing their communication and collaboration.

5.3. Strategies to Foster Openness

Building openness within a team is an ongoing process that can be fostered through various strategies:

1. Open Communication: Leaders must model open communication, encouraging everyone to voice their opinions.

2. Safe Environment: Creating a psychological safe space where everyone can express their thoughts without fear of retribution is key.

3. Encourage Diversity: Recognize and applaud diversity in thoughts and ideas. The variety brings richness to problem-solving.

5.4. Strategies to Build Trust

Trust, like a grand edifice, takes time to construct, but mere moments to crumble. Emphasis must be placed on several factors to foster trust:

1. Lead by Example: Display trustworthy behavior that includes reliability, competence, and consistency.

2. Transparent Communication: Maintain clarity and openness in conversations, especially on decisions that impact the team.

3. Acknowledge Mistakes: Foster a culture where admitting mistakes is seen as a strength. This will promote accountability and learning.

4. Show Empathy: Display an understanding of one another's emotional states. Encourage an ethos of caring and support.

Individually, trust and openness are formidable drivers of team effectiveness. Together, they bring forth an symphony of collaborative success. The intertwining of trust and openness forms a robust lattice of collaboration, making the team unstoppable against the face of any adversity.

By fostering both, a team can abandon their individual chrysalises and transition into a united force, mirroring the classic metamorphosis of caterpillars into butterflies. This process, although challenging and often uncomfortable, ultimately results in a transmutation into something infinitely more successful and resplendent. Making the effort to create such an environment is, therefore, not only worthwhile but also essential for success. Trust and openness are not mere accessories to be added for cosmetic makeovers of teams; instead, they lie at the heart of any team aiming to achieve shared mastery and success.

Chapter 6. The Science of Group Dynamics: Composition, Roles, and Norms

Group composition is the starting point of our exploration into the science of group dynamics. Without an understanding of the various roles that members play within a team and the norms that they are expected to adhere to, we might as well be setting sail without a compass.

6.1. Elements of Group Composition

For the uninitiated, group composition involves a delicate balancing act of skills, knowledge, abilities, and personalities. Diverse teams tend to yield innovative solutions and effective problem-solving, but managing these differences requires adept leadership. Assorted backgrounds can contribute to creative friction, but it also stimulates intellectual growing pains, pushing team members outside of their comfort zones to cultivate uncharted territories of potential. As members bounce ideas off of one another, the dynamism of their interactions generates a fertile bed for innovation.

Understanding the strengths, weaknesses, and aptitudes of individual members is key. Leaders must be like a master composer, expertly harmonizing the disparate notes of a symphony. A team with a balance of analytical thinkers, creative visionaries, detail-oriented planners, and focused executors will be far better positioned for success. This balanced team complement prevents the pitfalls of homogeneity while capitalizing on the diverse abilities of the members.

6.2. Navigating Team Roles

The roles individuals play within their teams can significantly impact the overall team performance. This is different from a job position or title; a role reflects the behavioral and relational aspects of a person's contribution. Sociologist Dr. Meredith Belbin identified nine team roles that individuals tend to fall into: Shapers, Implementers, Completers, Coordinators, Team Workers, Resource Investigators, Monitor Evaluators, Specialists, and Plant. Each role has a specific set of strengths and allowable weaknesses that contribute to a team's effectiveness.

For instance, a 'Shaper' is a dynamic team member who loves a challenge, while a 'Completer' is meticulous, ensuring the final output meets the highest standards. However, any of these roles in excess can lead to friction or inefficiency. Therefore, it's essential to have a blend of team roles for a balanced and well-rounded team.

In addition to these roles, every team member also assumes one of three social roles: task roles (focusing on the tasks at hand), maintenance roles (focusing on the social maintenance of group harmony), and hindrance roles (impacting group performance negatively). Competent leaders will ensure that these roles are adequately balanced to attain harmonious and productive team dynamics.

6.3. Norms: The Unspoken Rules

Norms can be seen as the hidden DNA of a team – the unspoken rules that govern team behavior. These norms provide the team with social order and predictability. They may include guidelines for handling disagreement, recognizing achievement, or setting work schedules. Norms can have a substantial impact on team behavior, determining how people communicate, cooperate, and confront each other. In essence, they form the team's cultural blueprint.

While norms typically develop organically, over time as team members interact, leaders can expedite the process by establishing and communicating clear expected norms. Remember, however, that implemented norms should reflect fairness, equality, and respect for all individuals. Building and nurturing norms centered around trust, honesty, and open communication paves the way for a highly collaborative and efficient team environment.

In conclusion, understanding and adeptly managing group composition, roles, and norms are critical components in the science of group dynamics. It is these properties that ultimately determine a team's ability to function effectively and achieve its objectives. Keeping one's finger on the pulse of the team's dynamics allows for dynamic, responsive leadership which, in turn, has a powerful impact on the team's capacity for fruitful collaboration and communication.

Chapter 7. Leadership and Its Impact on Communication and Collaboration

Embarking on the exploration of leadership, its implications, and the connected threads to communication and collaboration, we find that this intersection is one of the most crucial components that bind a team together. Leadership is not merely about designations or guiding others—it's a pivotal ingredient for fostering an environment of trust, open communication, and seamless collaboration among team members.

7.1. The Indispensable Ties Between Leadership and Communication

With the confluence of communication and leadership, a transformative synergy arises—an effect greater than the sum of their individual contributions. A leader's primary function is to guide, motivate, and cultivate their team's potential using effective communication as a key tool.

Leaders communicate the team's vision, articulate their strategy, and synchronize team goals. They epitomize ongoing dialogue, open-door policies, and inclusive decision-making. Oftentimes, the difference between a functional team and thriving one is the leader's ability to transmit a sense of purpose and strategic direction.

Communication in leadership is two-pronged: transmission and reception. Leaders transmit the vision, decisions, and processes, and in turn, receive feedback, concerns, and suggestions from the team. This constant receiving-transmitting loop forms the backbone of communication in leadership.

7.2. Leadership Styles and Their Impact on Collaboration

The leadership style adopted within a team greatly influences its collaborative efforts. Autocratic leaders may compromise open collaboration, as their unidirectional communication often quashes diverse perspectives. On the other hand, democratic leaders encourage participative decision-making and cultivate a culture of peer collaboration.

Transformational leaders inspire their team members to transcend individual performance levels to work towards shared objectives. They foster a collaborative culture, focusing on shared success rather than individual competition. Servant leaders create a cooperative environment by prioritizing the development of their team members, instilling trust and cooperation among the team.

7.3. Communicative Leadership: A Model for Success

A leadership paradigm has evolved where communication is pivotal—the "Communicative Leadership" model. The communicative leader focuses on efficient information exchange, fostering dialogue, and building relationships to ensure effective collaboration.

This approach instills trust, transparency, and mutual understanding throughout the team, laying a formidable foundation for enhanced collaboration. Communicative leaders, using empathetic listening and inclusive dialogue, create a space where every voice matters, thus triggering diverse collaboration.

7.4. Harnessing Technologies to Enhance Leadership Communication and Collaboration

In the digital era, leveraging technology is paramount for leaders to communicate and collaborate effectively. Digital tools streamline information dissemination, eradicate communication hurdles, accommodate diverse preferences, and promote team collaboration.

Leaders can use project management tools for transparent task assignment and progress tracking. Communication platforms facilitate real-time interaction between team members irrespective of their geographical location. Leaders harness video conferencing tools to humanize virtual communication and maintain a personal connection with distant team members.

7.5. Cultivating Leadership Communication and Collaboration Skills

The potency of leaders' communication and collaboration skills directly influences their team's performance. Leaders should strive to enhance their listening skills to comprehend team feedback better and to encourage dialogue. Emphasizing clarity while communicating minimizes misunderstandings.

Furthermore, leaders should foster an environment conducive to open communication where feedback and ideas are readily exchanged. Promoting team meetings, brainstorming sessions, and team building activities can enhance collaboration. Regular direct and indirect feedback cultivates an environment of constructive criticism essential for team growth.

The impact of leadership on communication and collaboration is multifold. Successful leadership depends largely upon communication skills and their capacity to collaborate. By nurturing these skills and using a strategic array of techniques, leaders can guide their teams to achieve greater heights of success. The combination of effective communication, tactical collaboration, and transformative leadership emerges as an unparalleled force driving team performance, worker satisfaction, and ultimately, organizational excellence.

Chapter 8. Harnessing the Power of Conflict: Alchemize Dispute into Opportunity

Disputes, disagreements, and conflicts are not inherently negative. In fact, they hold an immense potential for growth and development when harnessed correctly. The first step toward alchemizing disputes into opportunity lies in shifting our perspective and understanding the constructive, dynamic power that conflict holds within the realm of teamwork.

8.1. The Nature of Conflict in Teams

Conflict is a natural, inevitable facet of human interaction, and team environments are no exception. Multiple studies conducted over the years have further solidified this notion, reinforcing the inherent tendency for conflict to arise within groups. It's essential to understand that there's an array of factors influencing the prevalence and nature of conflict in teams. This can range from differences in individual perceptions, thoughts and experiences to contrasting approaches towards problem-solving and goal attainment.

Diverse viewpoints, varying perspectives, and a multitude of ideas can often act as the breeding ground for conflict. However, such diversity also paves the way for innovation, creativity, and adaptability. It's crucial to recognize the undeniable connection between diversity and conflict, and to perceive conflict as a resource to be utilized rather than a crisis to be averted.

8.2. From Conflict to Opportunity

The analogy of alchemizing disputes into opportunities is a profound one. Alchemy refers to a medieval chemical philosophy aiming to transform base metals into gold. By employing this concept to team conflicts, it suggests that we can convert disagreements and conflicts—often viewed as detrimental—into golden opportunities for team growth and improvement.

The process isn't as mystifying as it may sound. It requires the identification, understanding, and efficient management of conflict. Instead of focusing on eliminating conflict, which is an impractical and fruitless endeavor, the team should aim to harness the energy generated from disagreements and channel it towards positive outcomes.

The key to doing this successfully lies in cultivating an open-minded, respectful, and empathetic environment where dissent is valued as much as consensus and where every team member's opinions are acknowledged. Such an environment will allow the team not just to survive conflict but to thrive through it.

8.3. The Role of Effective Conflict Management

Effectively managing conflict requires certain skills and competencies—foremost among them being communication, emotional intelligence, negotiation, and problem-solving abilities.

Communication allows us to articulate our thoughts, perspectives, and expectations clear to the team. Without effective communication, misinterpretation and misunderstandings tend to seep in, further escalating the conflict.

Emotional intelligence aids in recognizing and understanding our and others' emotions. By keeping emotions in check, one can prevent the detrimental effects of impulsive reactions and heated exchanges.

Negotiation and problem-solving abilities are crucial when you seek a mutual consensus or compromise. They are needed to find a common ground and transform conflict into a cooperative problem-solving venture.

8.4. Incorporating Conflict Management Strategies

To alchemize conflict into a pot of golden opportunities, your team will benefit from employing various conflict management strategies. These could include adopting a collaborative approach where everyone works together to find a mutually beneficial solution or taking up a compromising stance where each party gives and takes a little.

Other strategies may involve facilitating dialogue, seeking external mediation, practicing active listening, and fostering a culture of feedback. It's crucial to tailor your approach to your team's specific circumstances and not stick rigidly to one strategy.

Regardless of the strategy you employ, the aim should always remain the same—to transform the ostensibly negative energy of a conflict into a constructive force that drives team progress and success.

By harnessing the power of conflict, you are not just resolving issues and disagreements. You're also democratizing the process of ideation, encouraging diversity of thoughts, and fostering an environment where every voice matters. This is the magical formula to transform disputes into opportunities. And with this strategy, your team will not just stay afloat amidst conflicts, but will also sail confidently towards the alluring horizon of success.

8.5. Conclusion: Alchemize, Don't Stagnate

The key takeaway is to perceive conflict not as a harbinger of disaster but a catalyst of opportunity. Teams must learn to alchemize conflict into resources for growth instead of letting it stagnate them. As you embrace the philosophy of converting disputes into opportunities, remember—alchemy is not an instantaneous process but a gradual transformation. Approach it with patience, grace, and resilience, and the growth of your team will be more golden than you could've ever imagined.

Chapter 9. Building a Culture of Feedback: The Importance of Constructive Criticism

In the grand theatre of team collaboration and communication, feedback holds a pivotal, yet often underrepresented role. It acts as a foundation for growth, innovation and personal development, while providing the opportunity to realign strategies, rectify mistakes, or build on top of solid achievements. Building an organizational culture that leverages feedback, particularly constructive criticism, can unleash the potential of team members while creating a resilient, high-performing, and adaptive team.

9.1. The Construct and Essence of Constructive Criticism

To truly understand the impact of constructive criticism in team environments, we must dissect its meaning and demystify its connotations. Constructive criticism is feedback that provides specific and actionable suggestions for improvement. Contrary to destructive criticism that demoralizes and disheartens individuals, constructive criticism is meant to challenge assumptions, encourage lateral thinking and stimulate personal and professional growth. It is poised, respectful and carefully formulated to avoid personal attacks, focusing instead on behavior, actions, and results.

Constructive criticism is, in effect, a path toward improvement, acting as a catalyst to instigate positive shift in team members' actions and performance. It is a tool designed not to inhibit, but to enhance; not to tear down, but to build up, not to discourage, but to inspire positive change.

9.2. The Role of Constructive Criticism in Building a Feedback Culture

In a vibrant feedback culture, constructive criticism is an unwavering staple. It fosters open and honest communication, encourages accountability, and perpetuates learning and improvement. By accepting and actively seeking constructive feedback, team members develop a mind-set focused on continuous improvement, rather than defensive posturing.

Constructive criticism serves as one of the building blocks of transparency in a team; it allows for realignment of expectations, clarity of objectives, and prevention of future errors. It instills a culture of respect where the inescapable imperfections of humanity are acknowledged, dissected, and improved upon.

A propensity for giving and receiving constructive criticism instills a sense of collective responsibility among team members. This turns feedback into a norm, diffusing potential defensiveness or feelings of inadequacy among team members, while making it easier for them to accept feedback, learn, and grow.

9.3. Delivering Constructive Criticism: The Art and the Science

The act of delivering constructive criticism can be seen as a performance balancing act amid the laws of sensitivity and honesty. Effective delivery of constructive criticism requires a blend of emotional intelligence, clarity, empathy, and respect.

One effective model for delivering constructive feedback is the 'Situation-Behavior-Impact' (SBI) model. The model suggests that feedback should comprise three components: specific situation or context, observed behavior, and the impact of this behavior. This structure can guide team members in providing clear, specific, and actionable feedback while avoiding undue focus on the person rather than their actions or outcomes.

9.4. Overcoming Resistance to Constructive Criticism

Resistance is a natural response when we are faced with criticism. The key to enabling a culture embracing feedback lies in transforming the perception of criticism from a threat to an opportunity.

One way to do this is to ensure that feedback discussions are rooted in respect and kindness, removing the perception that it's an attack on one's abilities or character. By using models such as the SBI and counterbalancing criticism with appreciation, resistance can be overcome, engendering a culture of learning and development.

9.5. Implementing Tools and Processes for Constructive Criticism

In the modern workplace, there are numerous tools and processes that facilitate effective feedback and criticism. These range from performance management tools, to feedback apps, to structured team retrospectives. Irrespective of the chosen method, it is crucial to establish clear guidelines on how to give and receive feedback, to ensure that criticism remains respectful, constructive and welcomes improvement.

In conclusion, constructive criticism is an essential ingredient for a robust feedback culture. It encourages personal growth, drives team performance, and fosters an environment conducive to learning and development. Establishing a culture of constructive criticism necessitates an understanding of its essence, strong emotional intelligence, effective delivery models, strategies for overcoming resistance and appropriate processes and tools. Embraced correctly, it can transform your entire team dynamic and set the stage for unprecedented success.

Chapter 10. Digital Collaboration Tools: Mastering the Art of Virtual Teamwork

First, let's embark on an in-depth exploration of the meta-concept which we entitle "digital collaboration tools" and the ways these instruments have come to revolutionize the landscape of teamwork in the modern age. The advent of digital collaboration tools has dramatically shapeshifted the ways of global corporate collaborations, harnessing the power of technology to bridge geographical divides and strengthen synergy amongst remote working professionals worldwide.

10.1. The Uprising of Digital Collaboration

Virtual teamwork, a collaborative model born out of technological advancements and evolving work cultures, has emerged as the heartbeat of successful businesses. The rise of global operations and remote staff engagement has challenged the traditional paradigms of a workspace, infusing new dynamism in the form of digital collaborations. Digital tools have not only demolished the geographical boundaries but have become the lifeline of successful collaborations in fragmented workspaces, connecting scattered teams and fostering a collective resonance through shared virtual platforms.

10.2. The Sphere of Digital Collaboration Tools

Modern technology has bestowed us with a rich plethora of digital collaboration tools, each designed to cater to specific teamwork facets. These tools encompass platforms for communication, project management, task inspections, video conferences, file sharing, collaborative documents, and brainstorming, among other things. Through these tools, businesses can orchestrate seamless operations, synthesizing different aspects with unmatched efficiency.

10.3. Pillars of Virtual Team Collaboration

An effective digital collaboration originates from the apt selection and usage of correct tools. Some of the key collaboration domains where digital tools have shown remarkable impact include:

- Communication Platforms: Tools such as Slack, Microsoft Teams or Zoom offer real-time communication channels, keeping teams connected and engaged at all times. Ephemeral chatbots, dedicated channels, and pinned conversations paved the way for smooth information and idea exchanges.

- Project Management Platforms: Asana, Trello, or Jira have surfaced as pivotal in organizing work schedules, tasks, and deadlines. Through appealing, user-friendly interfaces and systematic classification, these platforms enhance visibility and enforce an organized work approach.

- File and Data Sharing: Dropbox, Google Drive, and OneDrive provide platforms where teams can share files securely, and collaboratively work on them. Version control, access rights, and real-time editing features make these tools essential for modern teamwork.

- Brainstorming and Ideation Platforms: Tools like Miro, MindMeister, afford visual aids to facilitate brainstorming sessions, clarify complex concepts, and narrate stories.

10.4. Unleashing the Potential of Digital Tools

Despite a potent array of these tools, the successful realization of digital collaboration goals fundamentally revolves around their proficient use, appropriate tool selection, and adoption by the entire team. It is quintessential to curate an environment that encourages this digital adaptation, invests in training the resources, and promotes a feedback-intensive culture, driving continuous improvements.

10.5. The Influential Role of Leadership

The leadership in an organization plays a pivotal role in driving successful virtual collaboration. Leaders need to champion these digital tools, smoothly facilitating their adoption while ensuring no team member is left behind in this digital revolution. With the right balance between using these tools to track productivity and autonomy, leaders can create a trust-filled environment nurturing collaboration.

10.6. Challenges of Digitalization and Overcoming Tips

While digital collaboration tools promise immense benefits, universally perfect implementation often remains elusive. Key challenges include hesitation to adapt to the digital culture, miscommunication, lack of personal touch, and security concerns. Organizations can overcome these by endorsing a robust digital strategy, driving effective training, maintaining clear communication, promoting a balance between digital and human interaction, and investing in secure tools.

In culmination, the art of mastering virtual teamwork via digital collaboration tools involves a balance of technology adoption, responsibility sharing, cultural shift, and empathetic leadership. The measure, however, isn't the mere implementation of these tools, but their effective, lucid use and the resultant enhancement in team productivity and satisfaction. In the grand scheme of collaboration, these digital tools are not just the enablers but emancipators, leading teams towards unprecedented heights of success.

Chapter 11. Continuous Improvement: Sustaining Success in Communication and Collaboration

As we thread our way through the labyrinth of team collaboration and its multifaceted nature, we inevitably clinch upon the crux of ongoing success—continuous improvement. Teams are not static entities that, once formed, remain set in their ways. They evolve, morphing and adapting to new circumstances and challenges, and their capacity to do so effectively is pivotal to their long-term success.

11.1. Embracing the Paradigm of Kaizen

The oriental concept of Kaizen, originating from Japan, has permeated business culture globally, and rightly so. The term conceptualizes the ethos of continuous improvement in business operations, aiming for enhancement and perfection across all aspects of an organization's dynamics. The concept zeroes in on encompassing every individual in the process, from top-level management to ground-floor employees. To encapsulate this approach in a team collaboration context, we should inculcate a collective mindset that seeks to strengthen communication, streamline collaborations, and perpetually aim higher.

11.2. The Cycle of Plan-Do-Check-Act

An intrinsic piece of the continuous improvement puzzle is the cycle of 'Plan-Do-Check-Act' (PDCA), also referred to as the 'Deming Cycle.'

This strategy offers a systematic approach for teams to evaluate their performance, make requisite adjustments, and consistently improve their collaborative efforts.

1. Plan: At this stage, teams establish their objectives and strategize ways to accomplish their goals in respect of communication and collaboration. The planning stage necessitates an unflinching look at the team's current performance and identification of areas where improvements can be made.

2. Do: With a concrete plan in place, it's time for teams to spring into action, implementing the strategies and alterations laid out in the earlier phase.

3. Check: Having enacted the plan, the team then conducts a thorough analysis of the effects garnered through these changes. Appraising if the methods executed have indeed brought about an improvement or not is essential.

4. Act: Learning from the 'Check' phase, teams adapt their strategies accordingly, adjusting their future approach.

11.3. Incorporating Feedback Loops

Feedback loops—through which information output from an event or process is used as an input for further modifications—fuel the growth engine of teams. The role of constructive criticism here cannot be overstressed. Regular and structured feedback sessions help identify potential gaps in communication, misunderstandings, or ineffective collaboration methods. Such recognition of loopholes forms the backbone of future strategizing and planning, thus feeding into the PDCA cycle.

11.4. Nurturing a Learning Culture

A team that learns together, grows together. Teams must foster an environment that encourages learning from both successes and failures. An open-ended collaboration where individuals feel safe to share experiences, impart knowledge, and mutually grow, enhances the team's intellectual quotient and boosts innovation. A perpetual learning culture also expands the team's toolkit, empowering them with diversified strategies to approach tasks and overcoming challenges.

11.5. Capitalizing on Technology

In an age where technology has imbued itself into every facet of our lives, the potential of digital tools to support continuous improvement in communication and collaboration cannot be overlooked. Embrace project management tools, team communication applications, and other collaborative platforms to promote seamless collaboration, stimulate engagement, and fuel improvement.

11.6. Leveraging Data

In today's data-driven world, numbers hold the power to offer profound insights. Use quantitative metrics to gage your team's performance and progress. KPIs (Key Performance Indicators) like team productivity, timeliness, collaboration quality, and other specific variables relevant to your team offer a tangible, numeric frame to the often qualitative aspects of communication and collaboration. Data can aid in measuring success, diagnosing problem areas, and consequently, in chalking out improvement strategies.

Continuous improvement isn't a one-time act; it's an ethos that weaves itself into the fabric of your team culture. It presses the team to strive for excellence by ceaselessly augmenting their communication and collaboration techniques. A tactful application of the discussed strategies equips teams to sustain their success better and foster an environment where growth thrives amidst the winds of constant change. Here's to perpetually striving for enhancements and garnering phenomenal triumphs in communication and collaboration!

www.ingramcontent.com/pod-product-compliance
Lightning Source LLC
Chambersburg PA
CBHW071042260726
48661CB00007B/3113